In Summer

illustrated by
Marie Claude Monchaux

THE
CHILD'S
WORLD

ELGIN, ILLINOIS 60120

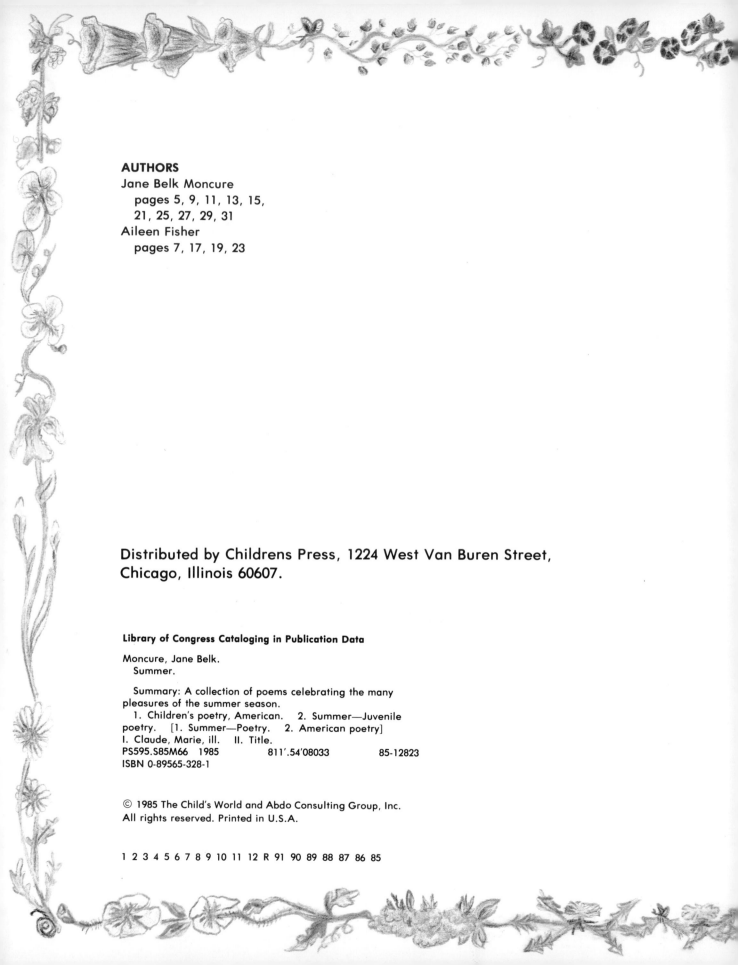

AUTHORS

Jane Belk Moncure
   pages 5, 9, 11, 13, 15,
   21, 25, 27, 29, 31
Aileen Fisher
   pages 7, 17, 19, 23

Distributed by Childrens Press, 1224 West Van Buren Street, Chicago, Illinois 60607.

Library of Congress Cataloging in Publication Data

Moncure, Jane Belk.
  Summer.

  Summary: A collection of poems celebrating the many
pleasures of the summer season.
  1. Children's poetry, American.   2. Summer—Juvenile
poetry. [1. Summer—Poetry. 2. American poetry]
I. Claude, Marie, ill. II. Title.
PS595.S85M66 1985   811'.54'08033   85-12823
ISBN 0-89565-328-1

1 2 3 4 5 6 7 8 9 10 11 12 R 91 90 89 88 87 86 85

In Summer

It's that sun time,
  fun time
part of the year
when swimming pool sounds
say, "SUMMER IS HERE!"

Summertime

Summertime is
swimming time,
bathing suit and
beach ball time.
I can go barefoot
every day,
I wish I could make
the summer stay.

Summer Morning

Mornings can be
   dazzling bright,
   when we've had
   a dewy night.
Sparklers blaze
   on grass and weeds,
   and spider webs
   are strings of beads.

When It's Hot

We raced so fast
through the woods and fields
to the pond
by the willow tree.
My brother won
and swam away.
Why didn't he wait
for me?

A Picnic

After the picnic,
my brother and I
played in the fields
where the butterflies fly.
I picked flowers,
and when we sat down,
I made a fairy-princess
crown.
Now I need a prince
and a castle too.
But my brother won't
play pretend. Will you?

Summer Clouds

There's a marshmallow mountain
   above my head . . .
   and way over there is a
   giant's bed —
   all puffy with pillows,
   fluffy and white.
Where do clouds go
   on a summer's night?

Sandbox Fun

"Dig and dump," I say to
    my hands.
"You are my steam shovels
    in the sand.
Build me a road.
Build me a wall.
Build me a bridge
    and a castle tall."

Rain

We stood and watched
    the rain, rain, rain,
    beat loudly on
    the windowpane.
And Jason said,
    "I'm thankful that
    our house has on
    a leak-proof hat."
"And," Pam said, "houses
    are so wise
    to wear those glasses
    on their eyes."

Swimming

I wish, I wish
I could swim like a fish.
Fish are so trim,
    the way they swim —
    with a dip and a dash
    and a flip and a flash.
But I . . . just SPLASH!

A Summer Chase

I wish I could keep my
   GRASSHOPPER GREEN.
But whenever I catch him,
he squeezes between my fingers
and flutters as if to say,
"You'll never hold me
on a summer day."
Oops! He's gone again!

Fourth of July

Everyone's excited
   on the 4th of July.
We stand along the sidewalk
   when the band goes by.
And then we have a picnic;
   we have apple pie.
And at night we watch the rockets,
   throwing stars across the sky.

Shells

Mom says sea shells
   were once the homes
   for tiny animals
   in the sea.
A shell could never be
   a home for you or me.
These shells that the animals
   left
   have washed up
   on the shore.
I'll just take them home
   with me.
The animals won't need them
   anymore.

Fireflies

The fireflies click on their
   tiny lights
   to brighten up the
   summer nights.
But, how do they click
   them on . . .
   and then,
   how do they click them
   off again?

My Swing

A swing can be anything
   as I go . . .
   up and down,
   fast and slow.
It can be a rocket ship,
   flying high.
It can be a bird, or a kite
   in the sky.
I don't need a motor,
   or wings,
   or a string.
I can fly high just by
   pumping my swing!

Bedtime In Summer

In winter when it's time for bed,
  the world outside is dark.
In summer when it's bedtime,
  it's still daylight in the park.
The sun still shines at eight o'clock.
  I see it in the sky.
If the sun can stay up late in summer,
  why, oh why, can't I?